Demonology

Sorting Fact From Fiction: A Field Guide Of Demons In Christianity

By: Riley Star

Copyrights and Trademarks

All rights reserved. No part of this book may be reproduced or transformed in any form or by any means, graphic, electronic, or mechanical, including photocopying, recording, taping, or by any information storage retrieval system, without the written permission of the author.

This publication is Copyright © 2015. All products, graphics, publications, software and services mentioned and recommended in this publication are protected by trademarks. In such instance, all trademarks & copyright belong to the respective owners.

Disclaimer and Legal Notice

This product is not legal, medical, or accounting advice and should not be interpreted in that manner. You need to do your own due-diligence to determine if the content of this product is right for you. While every attempt has been made to verify the information shared in this publication, neither the author, neither publisher, nor the affiliates assume any responsibility for errors, omissions or contrary interpretation of the subject matter herein. Any perceived slights to any specific person(s) or organization(s) are purely unintentional.

We have no control over the nature, content and availability of the web sites listed in this book. The inclusion of any web site links does not necessarily imply a recommendation or endorse the views expressed within them. We take no responsibility for, and will not be liable for, the websites being temporarily unavailable or being removed from the internet.

The accuracy and completeness of information provided herein and opinions stated herein are not guaranteed or warranted to produce any particular results, and the advice and strategies, contained herein may not be suitable for every individual. Neither the author nor the publisher shall be liable for any loss incurred as a consequence of the use and application, directly or indirectly, of any information presented in this work. This publication is designed to provide information in regard to the subject matter covered.

Neither the author nor the publisher assume any responsibility for any errors or omissions, nor do they represent or warrant that the ideas, information, actions, plans, suggestions contained in this book is in all cases accurate. It is the reader's responsibility to find advice before putting anything written in this book into practice. The information in this book is not intended to serve as legal, medical, or accounting advice.

Foreword

For 11 years, I cared for an elderly aunt who suffered a debilitating stroke in 2002. What began as the kind of short-term memory loss typical after such an event gradually became deep-seated and then violent dementia.

A woman who had been regarded by all who knew her as a nurturing, loving presence became a foul-mouthed, angry harridan. There were no filters left. Everything that came out of her mouth was filled with hatred and vitriol.

She abandoned any attempts at personal hygiene, and even used her own bodily by-products as weapons. Had we been living in the Middle Ages, I would likely have appealed to a priest to cast out what was surely a demon possessing her body.

Since we were living in the United States at the close of the 20th century, I was shocked when my business partner told me that she had been cautioned to break off her association with me. A family member who practiced a fundamentalist branch of the Christian faith told my partner that I could be a conduit by which Satan would enter her household.

The woman reasoned that the devil had infected my aunt, and would jump from her through me to corrupt another family. Or at least I think that's how the "infection" was supposed to occur. I was so shocked by what I was hearing, I didn't ask for the specifics.

Having witnessed my aunt's mental decline to the ravages of dementia, I can say, without question, that it is as if an alien being is in possession of your loved one's mental faculties. There were times when I could not believe what was coming out of her mouth.

I wasted hours trying to reason with her and to appeal to the person I was sure must still be in there amidst all that confusion. I know now that I was engaged in a hopeless endeavor, but never at any point did I think I was waging battle with the Devil.

In the months that followed my aunt's death, as I struggled to come to terms with many aspects of my long-term caregiving experience, my mind kept coming back to this suggestion that Satan had come into our home.

It was then that I really became aware of a growing popular perception that Lucifer is an active agent in the world and that mankind is locked in the middle of an epic struggle between ultimate good and ultimate evil.

This book came out of my personal research into a topic that at first I found both amusing and annoying. I am hardly a candidate for a remake of the pea soup scene in *The Exorcist*, but with no medical explanation of dementia, I came to see how possession would have once seemed a real possibility.

The perceived role of demons in the spiritual thought of Western society is a fascinating topic, and one that can provide a lifetime of study. I found the major stumbling block to be separating fact from fiction. The popularity of paranormal books and films, as well as a whole host of "scary" movies and TV shows has created a huge body of fictional demonic lore that, while entertaining, has little basis in theology.

There are plenty of people, my business partner included, who say it's all fiction, but I am a great lover of myth, a word I hasten to define in the text as an instructive story. You must get over the idea that a myth is something false to come at this material from the interpretational angle I am suggesting.

Deciding whether actual demons are real or not is, as they say, "above my pay grade." I do think, however, that evil exists in this world. It takes only a few seconds of scanning the headlines to come to this conclusion. Mankind has been attempting to explain evil and to deal with its presence for millennia.

This books explores that same theme, and is an effort to get back to more concrete perceptions of demons and demonology as expressed in Western Christianity. Whether real or symbolic, demons represent those aspects of the human condition and moral struggles that plague us all.

Table of Contents

Table Of Contents

Table Of Contents

Table Of Contents

Table Of Contents

Table Of Contents

Part 1 - A Theological Look at Demonology

What exactly is demonology? Like any word that ends in "ology," it's tempting to simply say, "Demonology is the study of demons," and be done with it. Unfortunately, understanding demonology as an aspect of theology is not that simple.

It is perhaps more accurate to say that demonology is the study of supernatural beings that are not gods. This can include spirits that might also be considered benevolent. The discipline varies widely by cultural and spiritual belief.

If, for instance, you believe in demons that are the minions of Satan, but have a strong attraction to a nature religion like Wicca, you might also believe in fairies, elves, sprites or other "spirits" that are considered "mischievous," but not necessarily "evil" per se. This book will look at demonology in a Western Christian context. It is not, however, a religious book in and of itself.

In the 21st century, more people have a passing conversance with demonology than you might expect, but much of that "knowledge" is derived from popular culture. While entertaining, and often frightening, this type of demonology generally has little to do with the theological study of demons.

Popular Culture Demonology

Television programs like *Buffy the Vampire Slayer*, *Supernatural, Sleepy Hollow, Being Human, Witches of East End,* and *Constantine* have given an entire generation a paranormal and demonic vocabulary.

Reality programs such as *Ghosthunters* often feature "demon hunters" like John Zaffis and Ed and Lorraine Warren who claim to overlay "fact" on fiction. Zaffis scored his own show, *Haunted Collector,* and the Warrens first came to fame due to their involvement in the Amityville Horror case. But how does this blending of entertainment and theology serve the popular perception of demonology? Often, poorly.

One of the most beloved characters in the *Buffy* series was a green-skinned "Deathwok Clan" demon with red horns named Lorne. He had more in common with a Frank Sinatra-esque lounge singer than a bloodthirsty creature from another realm — and zero credibility in terms of established demon lore. Lorne is a charming fictional creation, but he has no basis in fact. On the other hand, Moloch, the demonic bad guy that plagued "witnesses" Ichabod Crane and Abigail Mills in the first season of the Fox series *Sleepy Hollow* does have proper demonic *bona fides*.

Moloch is spoken of in the Bible, as well as in Milton's *Paradise Lost*. Long associated with child sacrifice, the series writers made Moloch's chief agent the disaffected and scarred son of Crane and his witch wife, Katrina. While granted a "mashup" of Washington Irving's original *Legend of Sleepy Hollow* and esoteric religious literature, the result is much more commendable than most such attempts.

In 2014, NBC made a demonic entry in their Friday night line-up with *Constantine*, an adaptation centering on a character from the DC Comic *Hellblazer*. In the series, rogue exorcist and demon hunter John Constantine protects the innocent and battles the forces of darkness in uneasy alliance with an angel named Manny. Keanu Reeves played the same demon hunter in a 2005 film adaptation also called *Constantine*.

In a review of that work published in the *Journal of Religion and Film*, Jeffry Mallinson, dean of the School of Theology at Colorado Christian University wrote:

> Audience members with any theological or biblical background will have difficulty willfully suspending disbelief. Much of the plot depends on a caricature of Roman Catholic theology where one is damned on a technicality or redeemed through a loophole. All of

this occurs without the satire of *Dogma* (1999)*. Particularly distracting are moments when John's Apocalypse is called "Revelations," and when an esoteric prophecy is found in a lost chapter of 1 Corinthians. The imagined text would have been more plausible as a Gnostic manuscript or secret copy of "Revelations." This may seem hypercritical; yet such distractions hinder the creation of a plausible fantasy world.

* *Dogma*, with Ben Affleck and Matt Damon, is summarized on IMDB.com in this way: "An abortion clinic worker with a special heritage is called upon to save the existence of humanity from being negated by two renegade angels trying to exploit a loop-hole and reenter Heaven."

While it might, indeed, seem hypercritical to take exception with the Book of Revelation being referred to incorrectly in the plural, the greater point is the ease with which scripture and esoteric texts can be used as plot devices with no fear of a discerning general public quibbling. The average "man on the street" would be hard pressed to pronounce much less correctly identify the origin of a Gnostic manuscript.

_____

Note:

Gnosticism was a 2nd century heretical movement in Christianity that taught a belief in the demiurge, a lesser divine being who ruled the earth, while Christ was seen as the emissary of a more remote and supreme being. In this school of thought, salvation or redemption depended on the attainment of esoteric knowledge or "gnosis.")

These same "men on the street," who would draw a blank on Gnosticism could undoubtedly identify "666" as the mark of the anti-Christ, offer up at least one paranormal story about a haunting, and likely assert the presence of Satanic worshippers among us. Never mind the fact that Satanists in the tradition of Anton LaVey, do not worship the Christian devil nor are they interested in being the evil counterparts of Christian churches.

LaVey's followers are, however, atheistic and materialistic. For them, Satan and demons are psychological symbols and representations of humankind's vital nature. Unlike teenagers spray-painting inverted crosses and burning black candles, Satanists rarely perform rituals. They do approach life from a skeptical perception and embrace unbridled devotion to sensual enjoyments of all kinds from fine food to sexual pleasure.

You can feel free to mix anything else you like into this "common knowledge" conception of Satan, demons, and evil. Throw in a little black metal music and Harry Potter for good measure. Few of the associations really hold together in a factual interpretation, but they do fit neatly into a fundamentalist religious filter that posits a cosmic battle between the ultimate good, God, and the ultimate evil, Satan. This view has, however, evolved over many centuries of debate about what actually constitutes good and evil.

Before we go on, I want to say that I am content for the reader to determine according to their own belief structure, the role of evil in this world. You may see demons as a metaphor for the internal struggles with which we all cope and that have figured heavily in Western thought and literature. You may see demons as active agents of Satan on earth.

For the purposes of this text, demons will be presented, theologically, as creatures in the service of Satan. In this view, their role is to subvert man's relationship with God by trickery and potentially possession.

The overriding point of this text, however, is to separate "fact" from "fiction" and de-sensationalize the popular, "common knowledge" view of demons that does nothing but fan the flames of religious and spiritual fears.

The Evolving Role of Satan

Many impressive books have been written about the evolving role of Satan in theological interpretation. I especially commend to you *The Origin of Satan: How Christians Demonized Jews, Pagans, and Heretics* by Elaine Pagels.

While acknowledging that I may be going down something of a slippery slope, I want to offer at least a conceptual summary of the evolving role of Satan as it has come down to us in Western religious thought. Since all demons serve him, he is the ultimate bad guy in this story.

Anyone even mildly conversant with the Biblical account of the life of Christ knows that he went into the desert before he began his public ministry. This is recorded in both the

Gospels of Matthew and Luke. Jesus spent forty days and forty nights in the desert struggling with Satan.

To fully understand how Christian theology developed to accommodate the twin concepts of good and evil as polar opposite locked in a cosmic struggle, we must mythologically step back from the question for a moment.

Creating a figure like Satan that is the embodiment of evil is an attempt to explain forces of chaos and confusion over which people exercise very little practical power.

It is a mistake to assume that the word "mythology" means something that is not true. A myth is an instructive story. Taken in this literal definition, scripture is myth.

That does not mean that it is not true as it is held close in the hearts of the faithful. Other cultures however, have their own mythology, and those stories offer interesting corollaries to standard Western Christian belief.

The Story of Seth

In Egyptian mythology, for instance, we find an incredibly all-purpose "devil" in the figure of the god Seth. He was believed to be responsible for an impressive array of chaos and confusion. He was the ruler of the desert and of foreign lands, of storms and turbulent seas.

His powers were associated with natural catastrophes including earthquakes. He was seen as the opposite of all of the life-affirming qualities of his brother Osiris. Instead, Seth signified darkness and disorder.

Seth murdered his brother Osiris, cut up his body, and scattered the pieces throughout Egypt so Osiris could not gain immortality in the afterlife. The wife of Osiris, Isis, gathered up the scattered pieces and reunited them, helping Osiris to secure eternal life and to become the king of the underworld.

Horus, the son of Osiris, exiled Seth to the desert for eternity for his crime. Clearly, there are similarities to this story and to that of Cain and Abel in the Christian Bible.

I do not share this Egyptian myth to suggest to Christians that the account of events in their holy book is incorrect. Instead, this is an illustration of a different society attempting to come to terms with the duality of good and evil. This is a theme as old as man himself, and one that continues to capture our imagination and places us on the horns of societal and personal moral dilemmas.

To grasp the evolution of Satan as Christians know him today, it is also important to realize that the Hebrew Bible is much less monotheistic than the Christian New Testament.

Angels in the Hebrew Bible

Before the appearance of Satan in the Hebrew Bible, the text introduces readers to angels. These are celestial beings referred to in Hebrew as the mal'akim or messengers. For instance, it was a mal'ak that guided Moses to the Promised Land.

These messengers might deliver the word of God to a prophet, assign a special task to a chosen person, announce a significant birth, guide an individual toward the correct path, offer comfort, or administer punishment.

Not all of these messengers, however, behaved appropriately, or we would not have the story of the sons of God who seduced human women leading to the birth of the race of giants called the Nephilim.

Basically, the Hebrews made accommodations for good and bad angels. The fully formed idea of demons only develops later in the tradition of the Christian faith. This is not to say however that there are not mentions of demons in the Hebrew Bible*, although the references are problematic in light of the belief that Christians hold today.

Note:

The term "Hebrew Bible" refers to the collection of Jewish texts that are used as the canonical sources for the Christian Old Testament. Most are in Biblical Hebrew with some Biblical Aramaic. The content is not the source for the canonical portions of the Roman Catholic Old Testament. "Hebrew Bible" is meant to be a scholarly neutral term with no implication of interpretative tradition.

As a comparison, the 46 books of the Catholic Old Testament are:

Genesis, Exodus, Leviticus, Numbers, Deuteronomy, Joshua, Judges, Ruth, 1 Samuel, 2 Samuel, 1 Kings, 2 Kings, 1 Chronicles, 2 Chronicles, Ezra, Nehemiah, Tobit, Judith, Esther, 1 Maccabees, 2 Maccabees, Job, Psalms, Proverbs, Ecclesiastes, Song of Songs, Wisdom, Sirach, Isaiah, Jeremiah, Lamentations, Baruch, Ezekiel, Daniel, Hosea, Joel, Amos, Obadiah, Jonah, Micah, Nahum, Habakkuk, Zephaniah, Haggai, Zechariah, Malachi

In the Christian Old Testament, the 39 books are:

Genesis, Exodus, Leviticus, Numbers, Deuteronomy, Joshua, Judges, Ruth, 1 Samuel, 2 Samuel, 1 Kings, 2 Kings, 1 Chronicles, 2 Chronicles, Ezra, Nehemiah, Esther, Job, Psalms, Proverbs, Ecclesiastes, Song of Solomon, Isaiah, Jeremiah, Lamentations, Ezekiel, Daniel, Hosea, Joel, Amos, Obadiah, Jonah, Micah, Nahum, Habakkuk,, Zephaniah, Haggai, Zechariah, Malachi

Where the names of other ancient texts are used in this book, I will try to identify them individually.

_____

In Leviticus, there are references to a demon named Azazel. It would appear in the text that Aaron sacrifices a goat to Yahweh and another to the demon. The King James version of the Bible gets around this by saying that Azazel is a place name, but it is quite clear in Jewish literature that Azazel is the name of a demon.

He is credited with teaching humans to make knives, swords, and shields. In the Book of Enoch, an ancient Jewish text but not a canonical book of the Bible, Azazel reveals the internal secrets of heaven and teaches man all forms of oppression upon the earth. Azazel also becomes transformed into the serpent that tempts Adam and Eve in the garden.

Another demon from ancient Jewish literature is Lilith who in later tradition is regarded as the first wife of Adam. She is found in the company of unclean animals and is in league with the head of the fallen angels, her husband Sammael.

Lilith actively works for the expulsion of Adam and Eve from the garden and in some traditions she is the servant responsible for the temptation story in Genesis. Following the expulsion, Lilith continues her attacks on mankind, and is generally held to be responsible when small children die.

The Hebrew text, particularly in the book of Isaiah, makes it clear that God is responsible for both good and evil. Satan, on the other hand, is a part of God's council. He is the Accuser, who serves at God's request.

The best illustration of this role occurs in the Book of Job. Basically, God throws Job under the bus to test him. When seen in this light, the story is the tale of God and Satan working together to put Job and his faith under the microscope.

The Personification of Satan

It is not the purpose of this text to fully explore Hebrew theology. If it were, it would become increasingly clear that Satan is an ambiguous figure as is his role on God's council. It would seem that Satan is an obedient servant of God, sending evil and misfortune to the unfaithful and the faithful.

There is none of the familiar imagery of modern Christianity that shows Satan as the supreme ruler of hell, sitting at the head of an army of demons for the purpose of waging war against God and humanity.

Grasping the familiar personification of Satan, requires looking to the period between the time when the last of the Hebrew Scriptures were composed, and the beginning of the life of Christ. This is generally taken as being 300 years in duration. During this time Satan, as we know him, came into his own.

These 300 years are referred to as the Babylonian Captivity. They begin with the fall of Jerusalem in 586 BC to the Babylonians followed by the exile of the Hebrews throughout the region. During this exile, the Hebrew people came into contact with Persian and Zoroastrian religious practices.

The evolution of Jewish literary expression subsequently transformed angels from "messengers" into distinct celestial beings with personalities and given names. Religious writers began to imagine a heavenly world which was much more elaborate.

The absolute dichotomy of good versus evil began to take shape. The word demon assumed a growing negative connotation for the Jews. These creatures were seen as being in league with an arch enemy who stood in opposition to the true God. Their role was to entice humans to stray from their faith. Demons excelled at tempting mankind and at promulgating false doctrines.

Thus, both the Jewish and then the Christian faith developed a working concept of a spiritual war. The conflict was, however, expected to come to a resolution on the Day of Judgment when evil fell before the power of ultimate good. Until that happens, specific demons are free to wreak havoc through spreading misfortune, cultivating sin, and exploiting the flaws of mankind.

What are Demons According to the Bible?

The Biblical interpretation is that demons are the fallen angels exiled from heaven with Satan as described in Revelation 12:9:

> "And the great dragon was cast out, that old serpent, called the Devil, and Satan, which deceiveth the whole world: he was cast out into the earth, and his angels were cast out with him." (KJV)

About one third of the angels are believed to have gone with Satan. In Job 28:4-7, we learn that angels were created before the earth and that Satan fell from grace before God tempted Adam and Eve in the Garden of Eden as described in Genesis 3:1-14.

Satan's fall is also described in Isaiah 14:12–15, which is one of the more poetic renditions of the story:

> (12) How art thou fallen from heaven, O Lucifer, son of the morning! how art thou cut down to the ground, which didst weaken the nations!
>
> (13) For thou hast said in thine heart, I will ascend into heaven, I will exalt my throne above the stars of God: I will sit also upon the mount of the congregation, in the sides of the north:
>
> (14) I will ascend above the heights of the clouds; I will be like the most High.
>
> (15) Yet thou shalt be brought down to hell, to the sides of the pit. (KJV)

In the Book of Jude 1:6-7, the sins of the angels are likened to the sins of Sodom and Gomorrah, in particular, the pursuit of unnatural desires. Genesis 6: 1-4 touches on this:

> (1) And it came to pass, when men began to multiply on the face of the earth, and daughters were born unto them,

(2) That the sons of God saw the daughters of men that they were fair; and they took them wives of all which they chose.

(3) And the Lord said, My spirit shall not always strive with man, for that he also is flesh: yet his days shall be an hundred and twenty years.

(4) There were giants in the earth in those days; and also after that, when the sons of God came in unto the daughters of men, and they bare children to them, the same became mighty men which were of old, men of renown.

These "giants," also called the "fallen ones" are the "Nephilim." Their story is the precursor to the Great Flood and Noah's Ark.

Demons are bent on using deception to circumvent the relationship between God and man. Whether that deception is simply by placing doubt in the minds of men or actually intervening in the lives of men via possession and other evil acts is a matter of debate. The Bible does say that demons can take human form:

> And no wonder, for Satan himself masquerades as an angel of light. It is not surprising, then, if his servants also masquerade as servants of righteousness. Their end will be what their actions deserve. - 2 Corinthians 11: 14-15 (KJV)

In other parts of the New Testament, demons are referred to as "unclean" and "evil spirits." They are said to do battle with the angels and to attack Christians.

Demons are characterized as powerful, the enemies of both God and humanity, but interestingly they are described as enemies that have been defeated. Satan is perceived to be the "prince of the world," but he is not portrayed in any way as being more powerful than or even equal to God.

Such an interpretation today represents a more fundamentalist branch of Christianity — and can even be found in some Satanist demonologies that reverse the balance of power and try to make Jesus a symbol of weakness and defeat.

Traditionally, good and evil are not equal adversaries in Christian thought. Satan and his demons are only free to work their trickery on earth until Judgment Day. There is no option for any demonic victory when Christ returns. Satan is a rebel angel who leads rebellious spirits on earth.

What about Demonic Possession?

There are no explicit statements in the Bible about the possession of *believers*. In Matthew 8:28, the scriptures state that Jesus encountered two violent demon-possessed men. The demons confronted Jesus and demanded to know what he wanted of them saying, in Verse 29, "Have you come here to torture us before the appointed time?" He cast the demons into a herd of pigs.

The story dovetails with the idea that demons are free to torment men until the Day of Judgment and we have to assume that the two men in question were not believers in Christ, since they had never met him. So the answer to the question of demonic possession has to be taken in that context.

When the New Testament speaks of spiritual warfare, believers are cautioned to resist Satan, not to cast him out. Belief is therefore critical to protection. It is also important to draw a distinction between being possessed by a demon and be *oppressed* by one.

What About the Current Paranormal Preoccupation?

The paranormal is everywhere. Indy authors on Amazon love to write anything vampire-related. The *Twilight* books made vampire and werewolves sexy all over again. *The Walking Dead* took zombies into the mainstream, with people who never even took notice of the undead rabidly discussing the fate of their favorite characters.

Is all this interest in hauntings, ghosts, supernatural creatures, and the like evidence of demonic activity in the world today?

There is no reference in the Bible to ghosts. A person's spirit either goes to heaven to be reunited with their body at the time of the Resurrection or the spirit goes to hell. There is no option for a deceased person to return to earth with a message.

There are only two references in the Bible to a dead person having interaction with the living. In 1 Samuel 28: 6-9, King Saul attempts to contact the prophet Samuel, which God allows long enough for Samuel to judge Saul for his disobedience.

Then, in Matthew 17: 1-8 Moses and Elijah interact with Jesus, but they are not described as ghosts.

Angels do, however, move among the living unseen and they do have interaction with people. Demon possession can occur among non-believers, and demons do know things about which people are not aware. Satan is identified as a decider and the father of lies.

Several passages in the Christian Bible speak out against any interaction with supernatural or paranormal elements:

Deuteronomy 18:9-12 (KJV)

(9) When thou art come into the land which the Lord thy God giveth thee, thou shalt not learn to do after the abominations of those nations.

(10) There shall not be found among you any one that maketh his son or his daughter to pass through the fire, or that useth divination, or an observer of times, or an enchanter, or a witch.

(11) Or a charmer, or a consulter with familiar spirits, or a wizard, or a necromancer.

(12) For all that do these things are an abomination unto the Lord: and because of these abominations

the Lord thy God doth drive them out from before thee.

Isaiah 8:19-20 (KJV)

(19) And when they shall say unto you, Seek unto them that have familiar spirits, and unto wizards that peep, and that mutter: should not a people seek unto their God? for the living to the dead?

(20) To the law and to the testimony: if they speak not according to this word, it is because there is no light in them.

Galatians 5:19-21 (KJV)

(19) Now the works of the flesh are manifest, which are these; Adultery, fornication, uncleanness, lasciviousness,

(20) Idolatry, witchcraft, hatred, variance, emulations, wrath, strife, seditions, heresies,

(21) Envyings, murders, drunkenness, revellings, and such like: of the which I tell you before, as I have also told you in time past, that they which do such things shall not inherit the kingdom of God.

Revelation 21:8 (KJV)

(8) But the fearful, and unbelieving, and the abominable, and murderers, and whoremongers,

and sorcerers, and idolaters, and all liars, shall have their part in the lake which burneth with fire and brimstone: which is the second death.

The only way to be released from the power of Satan is by salvation obtained by belief in the gospel of Jesus Christ. No other attempts to be free of demonic activity will work without that belief.

At best, paranormal activity is just the work of charlatans exploiting human fears for profit or entertainment. At worst, according to Christian doctrine and Biblical interpretation, such events are the work of demons seeking to conceal their nature for purposes of deception and confusion.

The Bible does not deny the existence of a spirit world, but it does say that attempting to contact the dead on behalf of the living is a foolish and fruitless endeavor.

Part 2 - Considering Demonic Possession

Now that we have looked at the "rules" of Christian demonology, we must turn to the topic of belief in both a secular and spiritual sense. It is all well and good to say that believers in Christ cannot be possessed by demons, but of the many mental states of mankind that could be manipulated by malicious spirits, strong belief certainly stands at the head of the list. Let's take a look at a completely benign example.

When an acquaintance of mine was headed to a big-box, wholesale "club" store specializing in bulk items, she asked me if there was anything I would like. Since I was planning to put up a batch of preserves with the fruit from my small orchard, I asked her to get me a 20-pound sack of sugar. In a couple of hours she stopped by my house, and carried the bag inside, putting it on the kitchen floor.

Later that evening, I went to move the sack, and found it unbelievably heavy. That's when I realized my friend had purchased 50 pounds of sugar. I called her to ask what she had been thinking! In complete confusion, she said, "But I know it was 20 pounds." I responded, "Well, I'm looking at the sack and it says 50 pounds."

Her defense was that she was incapable of lifting 50 pounds and carrying the weight from the car into my house and all the way to the kitchen. How did she do it? Because in her mind, she was carrying 20 pounds. That is the power of belief.

Arguably, belief in demons and their ability to possess human beings may be all that is necessary to open the door for such possession. To pursue this line of thought, let's consider some well documented cases of demonic possession.

Possession in Colonial New England

A Puritan minister in the Massachusetts Bay Colony, Samuel Willard, recorded the possession of one Elizabeth Knapp, from October 30, 1671 to January 12, 1672. Willard exchanged letters with the well-known Puritan preacher Cotton Mather, who subsequently published an account of the possession.

At the time, Elizabeth, the daughter of a farmer, was 16. She worked as a servant in the Willard home. The incident bears a striking resemblance to those recorded in Salem, Massachusetts 20 years later known as the Salem Witch Trials.

The possession of Elizabeth Knapptook place in Groton, Massachusetts about 32 miles northwest of Boston. The town was infused with an overwhelming and strict religious atmosphere. Willard was known for delivering sermons that warned local youth to be cautious against the works of the devil.

When Elizabeth first began to exhibit violent episodes, Willard had her examined by a medical doctor. No explanation was found for her behavior, which Willard meticulously documented. She first began to complain of pain, taking hold of parts of her body and crying out.

She said she felt as if she were being strangled, but would also lapse into hysterics. This could take the form of either uncontrollable laughter, crying, or screaming. She began to experience hallucinations, saying she saw sought two individuals walking around her.

Elizabeth claimed a man was floating around her bed. She frequently broke into nocturnal fits, falling into convulsions on the floor. She also tried to throw herself into the fire. At times, it took four people to hold her down.

On November 2, 1671, Elizabeth confessed to Willard that she met with the devil over a period of three years, during which he promised her she would remain forever young, have an easy life, see the world, and possess wealth. She claims to have signed a blood covenant in a book signed by other women as well.

For the rest of November and into December Elizabeth continued to have violent fits during which she would make animal sounds and speak in an odd, deep voice. Also during this time, she claimed to have visions of the devil. On the night of November 28, one of these episodes began and continued for 48 hours, throwing the girl into a catatonic state that lasted until December 8.

Willard made his last journal entry on January 15. There is no record of what happened to Elizabeth Knapp. Willard went on to deliver powerful sermons in Salem during the witch trials in 1692, and is also responsible for discrediting evidence against several of the women during the proceedings.

There have been many historical and psychological theories about the events that took place in the case of Elizabeth Knapp and during the subsequent Salem witch trials. The strict religious atmosphere of the period is often cited as being mentally and physically oppressive. The only acts of rebellion available to repressed young women were those that could be expressed in the religious language of the period.

Additionally, the young girls may have been rebelling against their limited place in society. Although the attention was certainly negative and ultimately very dangerous, being the victims of possession did elevate them out of the mundane and into a place of recognition in Puritan society they would otherwise never have attained.

The Demon of Murder?

Michael and Christine Taylor were a religious couple living in Ossett, England. In 1974 while attending a prayer group led by Marie Robinson, Christine accused Michael and Marie of having an affair. Although both parties denied the allegation, Michael began to act very strangely.

His actions, including extreme profanity, were completely out of character. The bizarre behavior continued for months, until Michael consulted with a clergyman who opted to perform an exorcism that lasted for more than 24 hours.

Oddly enough, although the priests claimed they drove 40 demons from his body, they allowed Michael to leave with the "demon of murder" lying dormant in his soul. The man proceeded to return to his home, where he killed both his wife and the family dog.

Authorities later located Michael covered in blood wandering the streets. At his trial, he was found not guilty by reason of insanity.

The Real Story of the Exorcist

Actress Linda Blair's portrayal of a child possessed by a demon in the 1974 film *The Exorcist* is so famous it is now part of popular culture. The story was based on an actual case that occurred in Cottage City, Maryland in the late 1940s. The child in question was a boy, best known by the pseudonym Roland Doe.

As the story is told, the boy's Aunt Harriet introduced him to a Ouija board. Upon her death, strange events began to occur. Furniture moving and the sound of marching feet could be heard throughout the house. Witnesses saw a vase levitate, a container of holy water smash to the floor, and a picture of Christ shake as though it were being hit from behind.

The Rev. Edward Hughes, a Catholic priest, ultimately attempted an exorcism, but was wounded in the process suffering an injury that required stitches. Later, three Jesuit priests attempted second exorcism. During that event, the words "hell" and "evil" appeared to be carved into the child's body. In total, 30 rites of exorcism were performed before Roland was able to lead a normal life.

The Most Famous American Exorcism

Anna Ecklund was born in 1882. A devout Catholic, she began to show symptoms of potential demonic possession in 1908 at age 14. She could not enter a church or tolerate being in the presence of any blessed or sacred object. She also developed an obsessive preoccupation with sexual acts that were depraved and disturbing.

This fact has been largely credited to a suspected incestuous relationship with her father, Jacob, although no conclusive evidence of this fact exists. By the time Anna was 26 years old, she was believed to be completely under the control of a demon inhabiting her body.

Rumors associated with the case insisted that her Aunt Mina, who was also Jacob's mistress, was a witch practicing the black arts. Both the father and the aunt were thought to be casting spells on Anna, which prevented the initial exorcism from being successful.

According to scripture, if a demon is expelled, but then successfully re-enters the body of its victim, he comes with seven additional demons stronger than himself. Thus, each case of repossession is harder to resolve.

Twenty years after the first exorcism was performed on Anna, multiple demons were said to be expelled from her body. The 23-day exorcism was performed at a nearby convent. During that time, Anna levitated, jumped on to walls in a crouching position defying gravity, and spoke in multiple languages.

Her body elongated at times and swelled. She displayed hidden knowledge and recited sins committed by those present during their childhoods. Horrible smells invaded the room, along with swarms of mosquitoes and flies. The presiding priest, Father Theophilus, recorded that he saw both Lucifer and Beelzebub in the room.

In his book, *Begone Satan!*, Rev. Carl Vogl wrote:

> Then, too, her whole body became so horribly disfigured that the regular contour of her body vanished. Her pale, deathlike and emaciated head, often assuming the size of an inverted water pitcher, became as red as glowing embers. Her eyes protruded out of their sockets, her lips swelled up to proportions equaling the size of hands, and her thin emaciated body was bloated to such enormous size that the pastor and some of the Sisters drew back out of fright, thinking that the woman would be torn to pieces and burst asunder. At times her abdominal region and extremities became as hard as iron and stone. In such instances the weight of her body pressed into the iron bedstead so that the iron rods of the bed bent to the floor.

On the morning of December 23, 1928, the exorcism was judged a success. Within one year, all of the nuns who had been present, traumatized by the event, requested a transfer to other convents. Anna herself returned to the convent four months later to make a novena of thanksgiving. During that time, she told one of the priests that the blessed Lord appeared to her frequently and encouraged her to remain faithful.

A Classic Case from 1906

The case of Clara Germana Cele occurred in Natal, South Africa in 1906. It contained all the classic elements of a recognized demonic possession. The 16-year-old girl reputedly had the ability to speak in multiple languages to which she had never been exposed.

She knew intimate secrets about individuals with whom she has no acquaintance. She levitated, and displayed unnatural physical strength, throwing about people much larger than herself.

Being in the presence of blessed objects was excruciating for Clara. Her voice took on a guttural, unnatural tone described by witnesses as sounding like a herd of wild beasts. When her priest was consulted, he revealed that Clara confessed to him that she had entered into a pact with Satan, thus allowing herself to be possessed by a demon.

Two priests conducted an exorcism that lasted for two days before they were able to drive the demonic spirit from the child's body.

Possession or Mental Illness?

In March 2012, Dr. Richard E Gallagher, an associate professor at New York Medical College was contacted by a local church about a woman who claimed to be practicing occult powers. The woman, known as Julia, entered trances during which she used multiple voices to utter viciously hateful phrases. Afterwards, she said she had no memory of the event.

This alone, was not enough to suggest a possession might be occurring. However, when Gallagher spoke with colleagues consulting on the case, the same voices interrupted the phone conversations.

At the same time, Julia began to exhibit seemingly psychic abilities. She knew personal details about members of the hospital staff and had knowledge of events that occurred in their homes that she did not witness.

During the subsequent exorcism, the temperature of the room became unbearable. The woman spoke in both Spanish and Latin, languages that she did not know. When sprinkled with holy water, she screamed.

However, when normal water was exchanged for the holy water, she showed no reaction. For approximately 30 minutes, she levitated. The exorcism was a failure, and Julia was not cured of the strange forces that appeared to be working on her.

The Children of Latoya Ammon

If you believe that demonic possession is something that only occurred in another age and time consider the story of Latoya Ammons and her children. In January 2014 in Indianapolis, Indiana the mother of three reported to local police that demons were possessing her children, then ages 7, 9, and 12.

Authorities were initially skeptical. However, after investigation and interviews that generated 800 pages of official documentation, even the police had to admit something unusual and perhaps even supernatural was taking place in the home.

The strange events began in November 2011. Although it was the dead of winter, a swarm of flies gathered at a porch window accompanied by unusual sounds. Shadow figures were seen moving about the house, and damp footprints appeared on floors across which no one had walked.

In March 2012, the frightened mother witnessed her 12-year-old daughter levitate over her bed. The child only descended when the family prayed over her. Afterwards she has no memory of the incident. The 7-year-old boy was thrown out of the bathroom, hurled by unseen forces. The 9-year-old boy was observed walking backwards up a wall before he moved on to the ceiling of the room.

In the end, authorities took the children away from their mother under suspicion of abuse. However, one of the investigating officers took a photograph of the home with his iPhone. In one of the windows, a white silhouette resembling a human form is clearly visible.

What Do These Stories Reveal?

This section began with the story of a possession that occurred in colonial New England for good reason. The Puritans have received something of a bad rap in the history books. They were not dour and unhappy people. They were however religiously dedicated.

Part of that dedication was a daily injunction toward retrospection. The Puritans were among the world's premier journal keepers. They wrote daily to examine the state of their souls. Psychologically, this suggests they were in a state of hypervigilance against evil, and especially susceptible to a belief that demonic forces worked in their midst.

It is interesting that the possession of Elizabeth Knapp and the events 20 years later that led to the Salem witch trials, all involved young women. Destined for no other fate than to become wives and mothers, it is easy to believe that many young girls never expected anything exciting or interesting to happen in their lives.

Just because these young women lived in the 17th-century does not mean they did not experience teenage rebellion. It does not mean that they did not take some pleasure in shocking their elders. It certainly does not mean that they were saved from experiencing new and frightening physical and emotional sensations coming to the surface as their adult hormones began to surge.

There has always been an association between demons, the erotic and the forbidden, especially in societies with repressive religious elements. The story of Michael and Christine Taylor includes the potential of adultery. That of Roland Doe features a Ouija board, never mind that there is nothing mysterious about the game board, which was introduced as a toy in Pittsburgh in 1891.

The initial advertisement for the first Ouija board said that it would provide "never-failing amusement and recreation for all the classes." Now a horror movie classic prop, the Ouija board was the natural result of the preoccupation with spiritualism that characterized 19th-century America.

Spiritualism gained a huge following during and after the Civil War, driven by the grief of people who lost loved ones in the fighting. It was a tragic expression of an unfulfillable desire to communicate with the dead. The Ouija board was conceived as a tool to facilitate such contact, not as a means to open the gates to hell.

In the tale of Anna Eklund, we see not only devout Catholicism, but the specter of incest and family abuse. Again, this is likely the case of a young woman who psychologically could not deal with what was occurring in her life, and thus resorted to a religious expression to release her pain.

Both Clara Cele and the woman known as Julia may have been mentally ill. Latoya Ammon could have been covering up the signs of child abuse in her home. Regardless, there were witnesses in each of these cases who saw the afflicted behaving in ways they could not explain except in religious terms that included the possibility of demonic possession.

It is possible to go back through each of these cases and many more that could be cited to find doors through which demons could have entered. Remember, that scripturally, demons exist to thwart the relationship between humans and God.

Were the cases actual possession, or were they extreme *oppression*? That is a difficult distinction to draw, but in each of the cases the cause was defined in religious and spiritual terms and the solution was sought on the same ground. This begs the question, are there ways that we can protect ourselves from the activities of demonic forces in the world?

Protection Against Demonic Forces

In his letters, the Stoic philosopher Seneca points out that it is easy to remain a moral man if you never step beyond the door of your home. Unfortunately, life calls us to leave the safety of our dwellings, and in the case of evil entities, even the sanctuary of home and hearth does not always protect us.

There are many accepted methods to shield yourself against demonic forces or evil influences. Spoken ritual has tremendous power. The use of protection prayers erects powerful mental and spiritual barriers. The prayers can be used anywhere, at any time you need them.

The words do not remove demons or destroy them, but rather help to take away a demon's ability to influence a person or to create an environment where negative influence is possible. Protection prayers also prevent a demon from jumping from one individual or one space to another in an effort to elude detection or exorcism.

The prayers do not have to be a part of an established ritual to be effective. It is not uncommon, however, to light a candle that has been blessed before the prayer is given. This helps the person reciting the prayer to envision themselves surrounded by protective light.

The following are examples of protection prayers commonly used under such circumstances.

The Circle of Light Prayer

> The light of God surrounds me.
> The love of God enfold me.
> The power of God protects me.
> The presence of God watches over me.
> Wherever I am, God is.
> And all is well.
> Amen.

Prayer to the Archangel Michael

This prayer was originally issued by Pope Leo XIII whose pontificate lasted from 1878 to 1903. The pontiff intended the prayer to be used as protection during exorcisms against Satan and demonic forces. There are three versions commonly used.

Version 1:

Saint Michael the Archangel, defend us in battle.

Be our protection against the wickedness and snares of the devil.

May God rebuke him, we humbly pray.

And do thou, Oh Prince of the Heavenly Host, by God's power, thrust into hell Satan and all evil spirits who wander the world seeking the ruin of souls.

Amen.

Version 2:

Glorious Prince of Heaven's armies, Saint Michael the Archangel, defend us in battle against the principalities and powers, against the rulers of darkness, against the wicked spirits in the high places.

Be our protection against the wickedness and snares of the devil.

May God rebuke him, we humbly pray.

And do thou, Oh Prince of the Heavenly Host, by God's power, thrust into hell Satan and all evil spirits who wander the world seeking the ruin of souls.
In the name of the Father,

And of the Son,

And of the Holy Spirit.

Amen.

Version 3 is the original issued by Pope Leo:

In the Name of the Father, and of the Son, and of the Holy Spirit.

Oh Glorious Prince of the Heavenly Armies, Saint Michael the Archangel, defend us in "our battle against the principalities and powers, against the rulers of this world of darkness, against the spirits of wickedness in the high places" (Ephesians 6:12).

Come to the assistance of those God has created to His likeness, and whom He has redeemed at a great price from the tyranny of the devil.

The Holy Church venerates you as her guardian and protector; to you, the Lord has entrusted the souls of the redeemed to be led into heaven. Pray, therefore, to the God of Peace to crush Satan beneath our feet, that he may no longer retain men captive and do injury to the Church.

Offer our prayers to the Most High, that without delay they may draw His mercy down upon us; take hold of "the dragon, the serpent of old, which is the devil and Satan," bind him and cast him into the bottomless pit "that he may no longer seduce the nations" (Revelations 20:2–3).

In the Name of the Father, and of the Son, and of the Holy Spirit.

Amen.

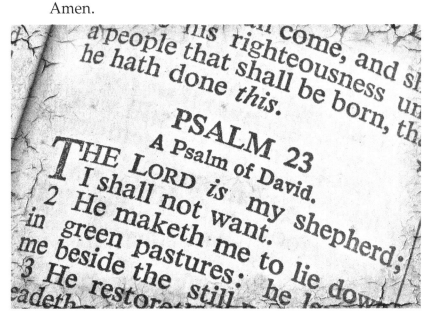

Sometimes, the recitation of a prayer is needed as much for the comfort of the individual as for actual protection against a demonic presence. Being anxious or fearful opens spiritual conduits through which negative influences may enter the mind and heart.

For this reason, the comforting and protective 23rd Psalm from the Old Testament is a popular prayer for many circumstances.

The Twenty-Third Psalm

> The Lord is my shepherd: I shall not want.
> He maketh me to lie down in green pastures;
> He leadeth me beside the still waters.
> He restoreth my soul.
> He leadeth me in the paths of righteousness for his name's sake,
> and yea though I walk through the valley of the shadow of death,
> I will fear no evil for thou art with me.
> Thy rod and thy staff, they comfort me.
> Thou preparest a table before me in the presence of mine enemies;
> Thou anointest my head with oil;
> my cup runneth over.
> Surely goodness and mercy shall follow me all of the days of my life,
> and I will dwell in the house of the Lord forever.
>
> Amen.

Prayer of Jabez

In a similar fashion, the **Prayer of Jabez** from 1 Chronicles 4:10 is also used:

> Oh, Lord that you would bless me indeed, and enlarge my territory, and that your hand might be with me, and that you would keep me from evil so that it may not grieve me. Amen.

Sacred Objects

Wearing or carrying blessed medals and other charms to ward off evil has been a common practice for centuries. The Medals of St. Benedict are considered to be especially powerful protection against demons.

St. Benedict was the founder of the Benedictine order of monks. The front of his medal shows the saint holding a cross in his right hand, while in his left he grasps a scroll bearing the rules of correct behavior for his order.

Behind him, a cup of poison symbolizes the story of a miracle ascribed to him. When a servant of the devil offered a poisoned goblet to St. Benedict, he immediately made the sign of the cross, shattering the goblet.

The back of the medal shows a cross and the letters VRS-NSMV-SMQL-IVB, originally seen on crosses hanging in the Benedictine Abbey of Metten. Their meaning was unknown until 1417 when a manuscript was discovered explaining they stand for Benedict's words when he addressed the demon who attempted to poison him. The letters represent his statement in Latin:

> Vade retro Satana.
> Numquam suade mihi vana.
> Sunt mala quae libas.
> Ipse venena bibas.

The translation to English reads:

> Step back Satan.
> Tempt me not with vain things.
> What you offer is evil.
> Drink the poison yourself.

In truth, almost any sacred religious object, especially one in which the wearer has great faith, can be used as a protection against evil. Such objects might include, but are certainly not limited to crosses, crucifixes, and rosaries.

Signs of Psychic or Demonic Attack

Some of the "standard" signs of psychic or demonic attack include the following feelings, events, or injuries whether felt by the individual or observed by others:

- An uncomfortable sense that you or your home is being watched.

- A sense of having been touched when no one is present.

- Hearing audible voices or inaudible whispers.

- Speaking in incomprehensible languages, or languages of which the person has no knowledge.

- Sudden changes in behavior and personality.

- A disruption in close relationships for no cause.

- Irrational emotions including anger, fear, and sorrow.

- Icy cold bodily sensations.

- A sudden and enervating loss of energy with crushing fatigue.

- Memory loss and "lost time."

- Confusion and an inability to make simple decisions.

- Recurring nightmares.

- Visions of horrific creatures and black shadows.

- Obsessive thoughts including desires and fetishes.

- Aversion to being in the presence of holy objects.

- Scratches, cuts, and welts that appear on the body without explanation.

- A deep sense of discomfort in given rooms or areas of a home or building.

In severe cases, affected individuals may appear catatonic, stare without blinking, or exhibit superhuman strength. They may foretell the future, or recite past events about which they could have no information without "retro-cognition." Instances of levitation and extreme bodily alterations, including change in hair and eye color have all been recorded.

House Blessings and Smudging with Sage

If you are concerned that evil has entered your home or family via any means, the typical first steps are to ask a priest or minister to perform a blessing of the house, preferably with holy water. Many lesser demons will flee a property when the name of Jesus is invoked.

There is also a more traditional, folkloric method of cleansing a property by "smudging" the house with sage sticks, which are readily available in most stores that sell bulk herbs.

Light the sage and move clockwise around the house starting at the front door. Use your free hand to gently disperse the smoke. Do not neglect corners, and smudge inside all closets. Include areas like pantries, utility rooms, and basements. If you so desire, you may invoke prayers of protection as you work.

If these measures do not work, you may need to seek outside assistance. In modern times, it is typical for medical and psychiatric experts to be contacted in cases where a person is deeply affected by some unseen force.

Unfortunately, science and the spiritual rarely come to a useful meeting of the minds on matters of faith. If all medical explanations for a person's behavior have been excluded and you believe demonic forces are responsible, you will be more likely to find relief consulting with your minister or priest.

Part 2 - Considering Demonic Possession

Part 3 – Demons A - Z

Since the word "grimoire" is derived from "grammar," think of the two books as having similar purposes. Both set out formulas by which fixed symbols can be used to form meaningful results.

For the grammar, that is the comprehensible presentation of information and thoughts in a particular language. With a grimoire the results are either the effective casting of a spell or the recitation of a ritual by which a demon is summoned.

The Lesser Key of Solomon is perhaps the most famous of all known grimoires, which includes an extensive list of known demons. It was compiled in the 17th century and is also known as the ***Lemegeton***. The text is made up of five books:

- Ars Goetia
- Ars Theurgia-Goetia
- Ars Paulina
- Ars Almadel
- Ars Notoria

The most obvious source for the material contained in *The Lesser Key of Solomon* is a portion of a book by demonologist Johann Weyer, *De praestigiis daemonum*, published in 1563. An appendix of that book entitled *Pseudomonarchia daemonum* was circulated as a separate work. It contained a list of demons and infernal spirits along with their titles and descriptions of the powers alleged to be attributed to each.

Weyer cited his source as the *Liber officiorum spirituum, seu liber dictus Empto Salomonis, de principibus et regibus demoniorum* (The Book of the Offices of Spirits, or the Book Called Empto, by Solomon, About the Princes and Kings of Demons.)

This work claimed that there were an estimated 7,451,926 "devils." They were organized in the 1,111 legions under the control of 72 infernal princes. According to the material, hell was arranged into a hierarchy divided into princes, ministries, and ambassadors.

De praestigiis daemonum came to be translated into English French and German. It was an influential work, even contributing to the 1584 skeptical book *The Discoverie of Witchcraft* by Reginald Scot, which decried the persecution of witches by the Roman Catholic Church as irrational and unchristian.

All copies of Scot's book, which attempted to be the voice of toleration were obliterated, however, when James VI of Scotland ascended to the throne of England as James I in

1603. The new king fancied himself to be both an intellectual and an expert on the subject of witchcraft.

James launched a wholesale persecution of suspected witches in Scotland in 1590. In that year 300 witches were accused of plotting to kill James, who nursed morbid fears of falling victim to a violent death. It was at this time that he also developed an unusually keen interest not just in witchcraft, but also in demonology.

The king's name is perhaps best known for his association with the King James version of the Bible, but the monarch also authored his own demonology in 1597. Today, it remains an essential reference source to understand witch hunting in the 17th century, particularly the trials that played out in Scotland.

Sorting out the provenance and interconnection of such esoteric texts as the few I have mentioned here is no small matter. As lately as 2001 a new version of **The Lesser Key of Solomon** was assembled from original and fragmented manuscripts in the collection of the British Museum Library. This edition, created by Joseph H Peterson, is considered one of the most complete and accurate versions of this famous grimoire to date.

Peterson joins a long and impressive cadre of scholars working to sort out the facts of the preternatural and malevolent. As early as 1486 a German clergyman, Heinrich Kramer, authored a witch-hunting manual called the **Malleus Maleficarium.** It, too, is considered indispensable for understanding occult phenomenon and the activities of demons.

This rambling bibliographic discussion could go on for pages, and is well beyond the scope of the current work. These books are mentioned to help the reader to become aware of the existence of a wide body of demon lore. The following brief descriptions of demons are drawn from multiple sources within that body and are offered for purposes of illustration only.

It is not difficult to locate books purporting to provide instructions for summoning demons. Clearly, as you read the descriptions in the following pages assembled from various famous demonologies, including **The Lesser Key of Solomon,** you will see that demons have the ability to tempt humankind with offers of remarkable gifts and great riches.

Although this should go without saying, the best way to avoid dealing with demons is to avoid any activity that could be construed by them as an invitation.

Many books about the occult are created for sensational entertainment and include spells and incantations without thought to consequences and responsibilities. If you begin lighting candles, drawing pentagrams, and chanting in Latin, you may wake something up that you cannot control — including your own fear and anxiety.

Some spiritual waters run dark and deep. Do not swim there lightly and with no guideposts. Even if you believe that demons are nothing more than symbolic representations of man's sins, flaws, and temptations, take care to put nothing in your mind that has the potential to fester and grow.

Abaddon/Apollyon

In the Book of Revelation 9:1-11, Abaddon is described as the king of locusts and the angel of the abyss. In Hebrew Scriptures, Abaddon refers to the "place of destruction," which is associated with hell. He is sometimes called the chief of the demons and in the Coptic Church is the angel of death.

Adramelech

In the *Dictionnaire Infernal* by Collin de Plancy, published in 1818, Adramelech is given three positions in the hierarchy of the underworld: high chancellor of hell, president of the high council of devils, and superintendent of the king of demons' wardrobe. He has the ability to transform himself into a peacock or a mule, and was worshipped by the Sephravites of the Old Testament with human sacrifice.

Agares

The demon Agares is described as an old man astride a crocodile who carries a sparrow hawk. He is associated with the teaching of languages, the return of deserters and runaways, the source of earthquakes, and the granting of noble titles. He commands more than 30 legions of demons.

Aim

Aim, or "Aym" rules 26 demon legions in his capacity as the Great Duke of Hell. Handsome and charming, he can assume multiple forms, using people's secrets against them. In his demonic form, he has a human head flanked on one side by the head of a serpent and on the other by the head of a calf (or cat). There are two pentagrams on his forehead. In battle he wields a viper in one hand and a flaming sword in the other, burning down entire cities at will. His preferred weapons, however, are cunning, manipulation, and wit.

Alastor

The demon Alastor is associated with generational sins. The Romans considered him to be the "evil genius of the household," and he plays a strong role in family feuds. In both Christian and Zoroastrianism, Alastor is known as the "executioner."

Allocer

Sometimes referred to as Alocer or Alloces, Allocer, as the Great Duke of Hell, commands 36 legions. He teaches art and the mysteries of the sky, inducing people into immorality. Allocer's face has lion-like characteristics with burning eyes and a ruddy complexion. He appears as a mounted knight, often on a horse with the legs of a dragon, and speaks with great gravity.

Amaymon

Amaymon (Amaimon or Amoymon), the King of the East in Hell, is a true demon. He was never an angel. Patient and full of resources, Amaymon possesses poisonous breath. He knows the past, present, and future, enabling visions and allowing people to fly. He supplies protections, provides familiar spirits, and revives the dead.

Amdusias

The demon Amdusias (Amduscias, Amdukias or Ambdusias) commands 29 legions in his capacity as Great King. Although he assumes a human-like form, his hands and feet are claws and his head is that of a unicorn. His voice is so powerful, it is likened to a trumpet but also associated with powerful thunder. Amdusias is the demon of the cacophonous music of Hell, and trees bend to his will.

Andras

Andras, the Great Marquis of Hell, sows discord among people and commands 30 demonic legions. He appears with the winged body of an angel, but with an owl or raven's head. He wields a bright, sharp sword and sits astride a black wolf. Andras has only one directive, to hunt and kill men. He is especially talented in using people's anger against them and infects humans with uncontrollable rages.

Andrealphus

Andrealphus, who appears as a peacock, is a great marquis. In human form, he teaches geometry and "cunning in astronomie." He has the ability to turn men into birds, and is the ruler of 30 legions.

Andromalius

The Great Earl of Hell and a fallen angel, Andromalius, calls 36 legions to his service. Depicted as a large man holding a serpent in one hand, he returns stolen goods to their owners, discovers wicked deeds, and finds hidden treasures.

Antichrist

There are four references to the antichrist in the Christian Bible, found in the first and second books of John. The antichrist is portrayed as a false messiah to be faced by Jesus during the Second Coming at the end times.

Astaroth

The demon Astaroth is depicted as a nude man with feathered wings. He wears a crown, rides a wolf, and holds a serpent in one hand. He seduces men by appealing to their vanity and sloth, always with "rational" explanations. Astaroth can make men invisible, give them power over serpents, and lead them to hidden treasures. He is regarded as the prince of both accusers and inquisitors.

Baal

Baal is one of the seven princes of hell in command of 66 legions of demons. He is believed to have the power to make those who summon him invisible. Baal may appear as a man, cat, toad, or combination of these creatures. Originally, he was mentioned in the Old Testament as a pagan god worshipped by the Phoenicians.

Balam

The great and powerful king of Hell, Balam commands more than 40 demon legions. He has the ability to make those who summon him invisible and to make them witty and clever with his perfect knowledge of the past, present, and future. Depicted with three heads (bull, man, and ram), Balam has blazing eyes and the tail of a serpent. He is seen riding a bear and carrying a hawk on his fist.

Baphomet

The name Baphomet first came into popular use in English in the 19th century. As a demon, he is popularly associated with an image drawn by French occult writer and magician Eliphas Levi called the Sabbatic Goat.

The image and its variations appear frequently in mystical and occult traditions and is an adopted symbol of the Church of Satan. The name originally described the idol or deity reputedly worshipped by the Knights Templar, one of the charges levied against the powerful group that led to their suppression in 1312.

Barbas

Barbas, known as the Great President of Hell, sits at the head of 36 demons and can answer truly on things that are secret or hidden. He both causes and heals disease, is skilled in teaching mechanical arts, and can assume human form. Normally, he is depicted as a great lion.

Barbatos

Barbatos is both a duke and an earl of hell in command of 30 legions in concert with four kings who are his companions. He can foretell the future, converse with animals, lead men to hidden and enchanted treasures, and act as a conciliator for rulers and friends.

Bathin

Bathin, one of the great dukes of hell, commands 30 legions. He can bring men suddenly from one nation to another and can impart the gift of astral projection. He understands the powers and virtues of herbs and precious stones. Seen as a muscular man with the tail of a snake, he rides a pale horse.

Beelzebub

Beelzebub is one of the seven princes of hell and his name, in popular culture, is often used interchangeably with Satan. He is also called the Lord of the Flies and is depicted as a huge demonic insect.

Belial

Belial, one of the most venerable of Satan's demons, was, according to the material contained in the Dead Sea Scrolls, the ruler of the dark side until the ascendence of Satan.

He is the demon of lies and a source of tremendous evil, commanding 80 legions. Some sources say he is the father of Lucifer, and the angel who convinced Lucifer to rebel against God, beginning the War in Heaven.

Beleth

Beleth, a terrible king of hell commanding 85 legions, sits astride a pale horse with trumpets and music playing before him. He is a fallen angel said to have been invoked first by Noah's son after the flood.

Belphegor

The demon Belphegor is one of the seven princes of hell. He seduces men by helping them to create ingenious inventions and to make discoveries that will make them rich. In some traditions he is the demon of the sin of sloth and his mission is to sow discontent and discord.

Berith

The demon Berith appears as a soldier clad in red astride a red horse in command of 26 legions. He wears a golden crown and has the power to turn base metals into gold. He also has the power to lend clarity to sound, including the voices of singers, and to make speakers perform with greater elocution.

Bifrons

Bifrons, an earl of hell, commands 60 legions. He teaches the arts and sciences, including the lore of gems, herbs, and woods. He appears first in monstrous form, and then assumes the shape of a man, and is known to move corpses from one grave to another, occasionally leaving candles or lights on the graves.

Botis

Botis, the Great President and Earl of Hell, is pictured as a viper, but can change into human form with oversized teeth and two horns. When seen in this shape, he carries a bright sword. He commands 60 legions and tells all things, past and future.

Buer

The demon Buer is also described as a Great President of Hell in command of 50 legions. He is capable of healing infirmities in men, bestowing familiars, and teaching logic, philosophy, and herbology. He is often pictured as a centaur with a bow and arrows after the fashion of Sagittarius, although he has also been depicted as a lion-headed demon with five goat legs.

Bune

Bune, another mighty and strong Great Duke of Hell commands 30 legions. He makes demons of the dead while giving living men wisdom and eloquence, as well as riches. Bune is often depicted as a dragon with three heads: dog, griffin, and man.

Caim

Also called the Great President of Hell, Caim gives humans the ability to understand the voices of various creatures including dogs and birds. He is depicted as a black bird holding a sword. Caim can assume human form, and in some sources is shown as a man, but with the head and wings of a bird. He also imparts the gift of future sight.

Cimejes

Cimejes, seen as a warrior on a black horse, is a marquis of hell in command of 20 legions. He possesses the ability to find hidden treasures and lost items and is known to teach grammar, logic, and rhetoric.

Corson

Corson is one of four principal kings (the others are Amaymon, Ziminiar, and Gaap) in command of 72 demons. In some demonologies he is the king of the west, and in others the king of the south.

Crocell

Crocell manifests as an angel who speaks in mysterious and dark ways. Considered to be a Duke of Hell, he rules 48 legions and is associated with the teaching of the liberal sciences and geometry. He can warm bodies of water.

Dantalion

Dantalion, the Great Duke of Hell, commands 36 legions. A teacher of the arts and sciences, Dantalion knows and can change the thoughts of people and can cause them to fall in love. He assumes multiple forms, both male and female.

Decarabia

The demon Decarabia is identified as a King, Earl, or Great Marquis of Hell. He commands 30 legions, and knows the powers of precious stones and herbs. He can transform himself into any bird with the ability to both sing and fly. He is often depicted as a pentagram star.

Eligos

Eligos, the Great Duke of Hell, rules 60 legions of demons. He knows the future outcome of wars, discovers things that have been hidden, and attracts the favor of important persons and rulers. He is pictured as a knight carrying a lance riding a spectral horse that may be winged.

Focalor

Focalor is a great duke shown with the wings of a gryphon. He overturns ships and drowns men in the waters, commanding both the seas and the wind. He sits at the head of 30 legions.

Foras

Foras, also called Forcas or Forras, is a teacher of ethics and logic. He knows the virtues of precious stones and herbs, and can make men more eloquent and witty. According to some sources, he can also give men the ability to become invisible. Known as yet another "President of Hell," Foras commands 29 legions.

Forneus

Forneus, a Great Marquis of Hell, teaches language and rhetoric. He can make men beloved by friend and foe alike, and can give them a good name. Forneus is seen as a sea monster, but can assume many forms, including human.

Furcas

Furcas or Forcas, a Knight of Hell, teaches logic, rhetoric, astronomy, philosophy, divination by means of fire, and palm reading. He is typically shown as an old man with long white hair and beard riding a horse and carrying a pitch fork.

Furfur

Furfur, the Great Earl of Hell, is known as a liar, never speaking the truth unless he is forced into a magic triangle. He can create storms with thunder and lightning and cause men and women to fall in love. Furfur is shown as a winged hart or stag and sometimes as an angel. His name is a corruption of the Latin "furcifer" for scoundrel.

Gaap

A demonic prince who assumes human form and incites love, Gaap teaches the liberal arts and philosophies. He steals the familiars of magicians, makes men stupid, and can impart the power of invisibility. He commands 66 legions.

Gamigin

Gamigin, a marquis of hell, assumes the form of a small horse, but can become human. He delivers accounts of the souls of those who have died in a state of sin and forces them to answer questions. He is also a teacher of the liberal arts.

Glasya-Labolas

Glasya-Labolas is also known by the names Caacrinolaas, Caassimolar, Classyalabolas, and Glassia-Labolis. A president and earl of hell in command of 36 legions, Glasya-Labolas is the author of bloodshed and the instigator of murder. He knows all the sciences and speaks of things past and present. He is seen as a winged dog.

Gremory

Gremory or Gomory governs 26 legions in his capacity as a duke of hell. He tells all things, reveals hidden treasures, and procures the love of women. He is, in fact pictured as a beautiful woman with a crown at the waist riding astride a camel.

Haagenti

Haagenti, a Great President of Hell, makes men wise. He can instruct humans in all subjects, transform any metal into gold, and change water to wine (or wine to water.) Seen as a bull with the wings of a griffin, he commands 33 demon legions.

Halphas

Halphas (also known as Malthus) is a rough-voiced Earl of Hell in command of 26 legions. Often pictured as a stork, he builds towers filled with munitions and has the ability to start wars.

Haures

Haures, also called Flauros, Flavros, Hauras, and Havres will speak freely of the fall of the angels. He can destroy the enemies of those who conjure him, and will speak of all things past and present. Haures is depicted as a man-like leopard with fiery eyes and powerful claws.

Incubus

An incubus is a male demon that engages in sexual activity with sleeping women in order to father demonic children. The female counterpart of an incubus is a succubus.

Ipos

Ipos, also called Ipes, is an earl and prince of hell in command of 36 legions. He can make men both valiant and witty and speaks of all things past and present. He is shown with the head of a lion the body of an angel, the tail of a hair, and the feet of a goose.

Krampus

A krampus is a horned figure common to the German
tradition. As a counterpart to Saint Nicholas, he punishes
misbehaving children during the Christmas season.

Legion

Legion refers to a group of demons mentioned in the Bible
that Jesus cast out of a man from Gadara and into a herd of
pigs. Mark 5:9 reads: "And He asked him, "What is thy
name?" And he answered, saying, "My name is Legion: for
we are many."

Leraje

Leraje or Leraie is a Great Marquis of Hell responsible for
causing battles and making wounds go gangrenous.
Sometimes associated with the astrological Sagittarius, he
commands 30 demon legions and is depicted as a green-
clad archer carrying a quiver and bow.

Leviathan

The sea monster Leviathan appears in the Old Testament.
He was used as an image of Satan in the Middle Ages,
threatening God's creation as the demon of envy. As such,
Leviathan is one of the seven Princes of Hell corresponding
to the seven deadly sins.

Lucifuge Rofocale

Lucifuge Rofocale is in charge of the government of hell. In modern demonology, he is thought to be one of eleven rulers in the infernal realms.

Malphas

Malphas, a Great Prince of Hell, is Satan's second in command, destroying the thoughts, desires, and strongholds of enemies and quickly gathering all the world's artifices to himself. He will accept any kind of sacrifice and sits at the head of 40 legions.

Mammon

In the Middle Ages, Mammon became personified as one of the seven demons in hell that correspond with the seven deadly sins, in this case wealth and greed.

Marax

The demon Marax, also called Morax or Foraii is a Great Earl and President of Hell in charge of 32 demon legions. He is a teacher of the liberal sciences and astronomy, with knowledge of herbs and stones. He is pictured as a man with a bull's head.

Mephistopheles

A widely accepted demon in Christian folklore, Mephistopheles derives from the German tradition, especially the legend of Faust who entered into a deal with the devil. Mephistopheles is also mentioned in Shakespeare's "Merry Wives of Windsor." Tradition holds that Mephistopheles comes to collect the souls of damned men.

Merihem

The demon Merihem is the prince of pestilence, held responsible for diseases and plagues.

Moloch

Moloch was a god worshipped by the Phoenicians and Canaanites who demanded child sacrifice. In Christian literature, he is used figuratively to describe demons that demand costly sacrifices.

Murmur

A Great Duke and Earl of Hell, Murmur commands 30 legions. He is a teacher of philosophy who has the power to summon the souls of the dead. He is shown as a soldier astride a griffin or vulture wearing a ducal crown and is always proceeded by the sound of trumpets.

Naberius

Naberius, sometimes called Cerbere or Naberus is a Margins of Hell commanding 19 legions. He has the power to make humans cunning at the arts and sciences and is especially skilled at speaking and rhetoric. He is also associated with the restoration of lost honors and dignities. He is depicted as a raven or three-headed dog.

Orias

Orias, also called Oriax, is a Great Marquis of Hell in command of 30 demons. He teaches the mansions of the planets and the virtues of the stars. He has the ability to change a human into any shape.

Orobas

Orobas, a Great Prince of Hell commanding 20 legions, is depicted as a horse, but can morph into a man. If conjured, he will be faithful to the summoner and will not permit any spirit to tempt him.

Ose

The Great President of Hell, Ose, makes men wise in the liberal sciences. If conjured, he can be directed to make any person insane to believe any delusion. Ose commands three legions and is depicted as a leopard with the ability to assume human form.

Paimon

Paimon, one of the Kings of Hell, roars with a mighty voice, but when conjured will answer questions put to him. He teaches philosophy, the arts, and science and especially reveals the mysteries of earth, wind, and water. He is pictured as a man with effeminate features riding a dromedary and wearing a crown.

Phenex

Phenex, a Great Marquis of Hell, commands 20 legions. A poet and teacher of the sciences, Phenix is a fallen angel who hopes to return to heaven. He is shown as a phoenix and sings with the voice of a child.

Penemue

Penemue is a fallen angel and was likely one of the healing angels called the "Labbim." He is said to cure the stupidity of men

Pithius

The prince of hell, Pithius, commands lying spirits and gives false prophecies. He is most often shown as a snake or serpent. The name is likely Greek in origin.

Pruflas

A Great Prince and Duke of Hell, Pruflas commands 26 legions. He leads men to tell lies and to quarrel, although he will answer questions truthfully if summoned. In addition, Pruflas generates poverty and sews discord. He is shown with the head of a lion or a hawk.

Raum

The Great Earl of Hell, Raum, commands 30 legions. Although pictured as a crow, he can adapt human form. He has the power to reconcile friends and foes, and to speak of things past and present, but he is also described as a destroyer of cities. Raul has a special fondness for targeting the souls of children.

Ronove

Ronove, a Great Earl and Marquis of Hell teaches rhetoric, languages, and art. He commands 20 legions and is known as a taker of old souls, coming to earth to take the souls of both humans and animals that are close to death.

Sabnock

Sabnock, a Great Marquis of Hell, builds and furnishes towers with munitions. He causes wounds to form sores infested with worms and to develop gangrene. Sabnock commands 50 legions and is seen as a soldier with the head of a lion riding a pale horse.

Saleos

Saleos, a Great King of Hell in charge of 22 legions, can find treasure, foretell the future, and locate hidden things. He is shown as a man with the face of a lion. In one hand he holds a viper, and is depicted astride a bear.

Shax

Shax, a Great Marquis of Hell, commands 30 legions of demons astride evil horses. He takes the sights, hearing, and understanding of men at the command of those who conjure him and will also steal money and horses. Shax is a liar, but speaks with a marvelous voice. He is depicted as a stork.

Sitri

In command of 60 legions, the Great Prince of Hell, Sitri causes men to love women (and women to love men.) He can force people to bare themselves on command. Sitri is shown with the face of a leopard and the wings of a griffin, but becomes a beautiful man when summoned.

Stolas

Stolas is a teacher of astronomy with knowledge of herbs, poisonous plants, and precious stones. He commands 26 legions and is shown as a long-legged owl with a crown, a raven, or a man.

Succubus

A succubus is a female demon that attacks men sexually in their sleep, causing their health to deteriorate to the point of death. The male counterpart is an incubus.

Ukobach

Ukobach, a minor demon, has a flaming red body, large eyes and ears, and is seen carrying either a hot poker or a pan of coals. The inventor of fried foods and fireworks, his job is to maintain the oil in the eternal boilers of hell. The oil is made of the blood of the damned.

Valac

Valac, the Great President of Hell, commands 30 legions. He reveals where serpents may be found and gives true answers about the location of treasures. Valac is depicted as a small, impoverished boy with the wings of an angel sitting astride a dragon with two heads.

Valefar

Valefar, also called Malaphar or Malephar, is a Duke of Hell. He controls the good relationship of thieves and tempts all people to steal. He sits at the head of ten legions of demons and is shown as a lion with the head of either a man or a donkey.

Vapula

The Great Duke of Hell, Vapula, teaches the sciences, mechanics, and philosophy. He commands 36 legions and is shown as a lion with the wings of a griffin.

Vassago

Vassago rules 26 legions. He is typically summoned to locate lost objects or to speak of past or future events. He can incite the love of a woman and reveal the location of hidden treasure.

Vepar

Vepar, another Great Duke of Hell, governs waters and creates rough and stormy seas. He can kill men in three days, afflicting them with wounds and sores that putrefy and breed worms. If asked by a conjurer, however, Vepar can heal instantly. Although referred to as a male, he is depicted as a mermaid.

Vine

An Earl and King of Hell sitting at the head of 36 legions, Vine creates storms, brings down towers and walls, and discovers witches. He is shown as a lion astride a black horse holding a snake.

Xaphan

The demon Xaphan was cast out of heaven with Satan and is said to have conceived of the idea to set fire to the heavens before the expulsion. For this reason, he is shown holding a bellows, which he uses to fan the fires of hell.

Zagan

A Great King and President of Hell, Zagan gives men greater wit, turning water and blood into wine and wine into water. He can turn metal into coins and give wisdom to the foolish. The commander of 33 demon legions, he is shown as a bull with griffin wings that can transform into a man.

Zepar

The Great Duke of Hell, Zepar, commands 26 legions comprised of inferior spirits. He excels at making women love men, but then makes the women unable to give birth. He is shown as a soldier wearing red clothes and armor.

Part 4 – Concluding Remarks

In this text I have tried to offer a balanced examination of demonology in the context of Western Christian thought. My own interest in the subject was kindled after it was suggested to me that my care of an elderly relative with dementia allowed the devil to enter my home, and potentially to jump from me to my friends and acquaintances.

While this assertion came from a well-meaning individual who espoused a far more fundamentalist religious view than my own, I still found it startling and unsettling. A long time-fan of the paranormal in both written and visual formats, I came to realize that a sort of reactionary popular perception of demons and evil permeates our society.

That body of "popular wisdom" bears little resemblance to the perceived role demons play in the celestial order depicted in scripture. Of course, there is even a trap in using the word "scripture" in a definitive tone, at least from a secular scholarly perspective. There are many versions of the Bible. Some books appear in the Catholic Old Testament, for instance, that are not regarded as canonical in the Christian Bible.

Discoveries like the Dead Sea Scrolls bring into question which books really should be gathered into any version of the Bible, since many of those text represent a second century heresy called Gnosticism. Of course, Gnosticism is a heresy because the Roman Catholic Church said so.

Did Gnosticism reflect the vitality of religious thought in the time immediately following the life of Christ? That subject is not the scope of this book, but it is a provocative field of thought. Again, I commend to you the works of Elaine Pagels if you are interested in pursuing a greater understanding of early Christian intellectual debate.

For these reasons, I have used the scholarly neutral term "Hebrew Bible" in reference to ancient Jewish writings, both those that did and did not "make the cut." In that body of material lies fascinating explorations of good and evil at work in the world and the role of Satan and the fallen angels in God's administration of the earthly realm.

Is there evil in the world? Yes. It takes little more than a viewing of the nightly news or scanning of the headlines to confirm that terrible things happen each day to innocent people. In exploring the source of that evil, I have tried to strike a balance between presenting a religious portrait of demonology and a symbolic interpretation of the subject.

As I said in the forward, I am also a great fan of mythology. Again, let me hastily repeat that a myth is not a falsehood. Myths are stories meant to teach us how to live in the world. Whether you view scripture as the divinely inspired word of God or a great work of literature (especially in the King James Version), the term "myth" can be accurately applied with no negative judgment attached.

If you look through the list of individual demon descriptions in this book, you will see that each is assigned a particularly deceptive and enticing power. They are given tools of deceit designed to allow them to lure men off the straight and narrow path. To enjoin a believer to resist the powers of any given demon is also to encourage that person to remain true to their Christian moral compass.

Is that the same thing as fighting potential demonic possession? The answer to that question can be both literal and figurative depending on your personal worldview. Regardless, the study of demonology offers a field for examining the extent to which we allow evil and negative forces to work upon our minds, hearts, and lives.

When we make a poor decision, even to the extent of committing a crime, the impulse may be the whisper of a demon standing behind us or the echo of an idea implanted in our thoughts from a worldly influence not in our best interest. The design of evil is to me as mysterious as the design of good, but I do not discount the existence of this ancient and cosmic struggle or man's susceptibility to its consequences.

When we pause to utter a prayer of protection or to reach for a blessed artifact to ward off evil, we may indeed be calling on the particular magic of faith or we may simply be taking a pause to weigh the matter and the situation in the crucible of our personal ethical scale. Regardless, it is in the space of that moral pause that a better choice can be made and a truer direction selected.

I do not believe that it is necessary to be among the ranks of faithful Christians to derive benefit from the study of demonology. If you are a faithful Christian, know that the fact of your salvation is all the protection you need from possession, and vigilance is all that is required to save yourself from demonic *oppression*.

I do not believe that my care of a dementia patient brought the devil into my home. I do know that the long-term caregiving experience exhausted me, and left me bitter, frustrated, angry, and skeptical. Exorcising those "demons" was necessary for me to move beyond the experience. Was that recovery divinely inspired? Again, I don't know.

I do know that in many moments of despair I found myself uttering the first lines of the 23rd Psalm. "The Lord is my shepherd, I shall not want. He maketh me to lie down in green pastures, he leadeth me beside the still waters. He restoreth my soul."

In arriving at your own answers to these universal questions, I leave you with a wish for still waters and a restored soul.

Part 4 – Concluding Remarks

Relevant Websites

Bible Hub
www.biblehub.com

Catholic Demonology
catholicwarfare.blogspot.com/p/why-this.html

DeliriumsRealm: Essays on Good and Evil
www.deliriumsrealm.com

Demonicpedia
www.demonicpedia.com

Demonology, Occult Phenomena, Exorcism
www.library.usyd.edu.au/libraries/rare/witchcraft/dem-occult.html

Demon Wiki
demons.wikia.com

Gods and Monsters: Ancient to Modern Mythology
www.gods-and-monsters.com

How to Protect Yourself Against Demonic Spirits
www.idiotsguides.com/religion-and-spirituality/supernatural/how-to-protect-yourself-against-demonic-spirits/

Internet Sacred Text Archive
www.sacred-texts.com

Jewish Concepts: Demons & Demonology
www.jewishvirtuallibrary.org/jsource/Judaism/demons.ht
ml

The Literature of Demonology and Witchcraft
digital.library.cornell.edu/w/witch/peters7.html

Mythical Creatures Guide
www.mythicalcreaturesguide.com/

Occultopedia
www.occultopedia.com

Roman Catholic Demonology
www.romancatholicdemonology.com

Spiritual Science and Research Foundation
www.spiritualresearchfoundation.org

Glossary

In most cases, a glossary is a compilation of definitions for words specifically used in a text. I have decided to deviate from that practice, and to compose something more along the lines of a paranormal and demonological vocabulary.

My intent is for this to be a reference source. This decision is based on the assumption that readers will continue their inquiries into paranormal, supernatural, and spiritual topics.

Like most specific subcultures, there is a "language" peculiar to such studies. Over time, you will become naturally conversant with this terminology. These definitions are intended to help you gain that fluency, but this section is by no means intended to be a complete or comprehensive dictionary.

A

Aeromancy - A means of divination that draws upon the shape of clouds and other natural phenomena.

Alchemy - The science of employing psychic substances to alter the composition of base elements for the purpose of transforming them into gold or silver.

Alomancy - A method of divination that involves the use of salt.

Amulet - Any ornament worn on the neck or wrist for purposes of protection or the casting of a spell by the means of inscriptions.

Animism - The belief that inanimate objects are alive and that they have souls.

Apantomancy - A method of forecasting the future based on chance meetings with various creatures including birds.

Archangels - There are four archangels in the heavenly host, Michael, Gabriel, Uriel, and Suriel.

Astral Projection - A process by which the soul temporarily leaves the body for the purpose of traveling on a different plain of consciousness.

Astrology - The study of the relative positions and movements of celestial bodies for purposes of interpreting their influence on the natural world and on human affairs.

Augury - A method of divination that involves the interpretation of signs and omens.

Aura - An aura is an emanation of light that surrounds a person or object that reflect's the individual's personality or the essence of the object.

Automatic Writing - Writing that occurs when the individual is under a trance and thus can be influenced by spirits, including demonic powers.

B

Babylonian Captivity - Three hundred years beginning with the fall of Jerusalem in 586 BC to the Babylonians. Followed by the exile of the Hebrews throughout the region. During this exile, the Hebrew people came into contact with Persian and Zoroastrian religious practices.

Banishing - An alternate term for driving away, casting out, or exorcising an entity.

Bewitch - The process by which a person is influenced via witchcraft.

Black Magic - That type of magic which draws upon dark powers including those of demons. Sometimes referred to as the black arts.

Black Metal - An extreme sub-genre of heavy metal music characterized by a shrieking vocal style set against fast tempos with distorted and undulating guitar riffs. Popular in Norway where it is associated with Satanic worship.

Botonomancy - A form of divination in which the future is foretold by burning the leaves and branches of trees.

C

Cartomancy - A of divination in which the future is foretold by the use of cards. A popular form of cartomancy is reading tarot cards.

Causimonancy - A form of divination that seeks to tell the future by burning objects in file.

Cephalomancy - A form of divination that seeks to tell the future and gain information by using the head or skull of either a goat or donkey.

Ceraunoscopyl - The use of thunder and lightning for purposes of divination and to gain information.

Ceroscopy - In this form of divination information about the future is sought by pouring hot, melted wax into a container of cold water.

Channeling - Channeling is a form of communication in which a spirit transmits information through a medium or psychic.

Charm - Any ornament worn on the body that is believed to be infused with magical powers for purposes of protection or to attract certain forces is referred to as a charm.

Chiromancy - Also called palm reading, this is the practice of divining a person's future by reading the lines on the palm of their hand.

Circle of Light Prayer - A standard prayer of protection used to guard against demonic forces or evil spirits.

Clairvoyance - The claimed power of a medium to foretell the future by examining happenings to come delivered in the form of visions.

Cleromancy - This of divination is much like rolling dice. It is the use of pebbles, small bones, or other odd objects that are cast and read.

Clidomancy - A form of divination that uses dangling keys for the purposes of answering specific questions.

Coven - A coven is an assembly of witches, traditionally comprised of 13 individuals.

Conjure - Conjuring is the process of summoning a departed individual, or any other sort of spirit by the recitation of an incantation. The word is also used loosely for the casting of any spell.

Cosmic Consciousness - When an individual has cosmic consciousness, they are said to be attuned to the vibrations of the universe. This is an expression that might be used by someone meditating, coming out of a trance, or even experiencing euphoria from drug use.

Crystal Gazer - A crystal gazer is a person who makes use of a crystal ball for purposes of divination.

Cult - A cult is any group, typically religious in nature that practices a set of beliefs and potentially rituals centering on focused devotion to a cult leader in opposition to mainstream religious or spiritual practices. The implication is that of a group set apart from the mainstream by rabid devotion to a charismatic leader.

Curse - A curse is any incantation or spell that is specifically formulated to bring harm or misfortune to an individual generally over a lengthy period of time and through repeated negative or painful events or circumstances.

D

Dead Sea Scrolls - Also known as the Qumran Caves Scrolls. A collection of more than 981 texts found from 1946 to 1956 on the northwest shore of the Dead Sea, a salt lake bordered by Jordan on the east and Israel on the west.

Demon - Although the term demon may have slightly different definitions according to spiritual tradition, in the Christian tradition a demon is one of the fallen Angels or associated spirits that exist to be subservient and obedient to Satan.

Demonomancy - The process of divination whereby the future is told and other information gained by summoning and conversing with demons.

Discarnate - A spirit that exists with no physical body.

Divination - Divination is said to be the ability to tell the future or to discover information that is secret or hidden. This is accomplished by a wide variety of methodologies from reading tea leaves to the use of Tarot cards.

E

Electronic Voice Phenomenon (EVP) - Any recording that captures voices and sounds that have not been heard by human ears and are believed to be communications from spirits.

Elf - A supernatural creature described in various fairy tales and folkloric traditions. Thought to be small and elusive with a human like shape, but pointed ears. Elves possess magical powers and are capricious in nature.

Exorcism - In the formal sense, an exorcism is a rite specifically sanctioned by the Roman Catholic Church for the purposes of casting a demon out of the body of a possessed individual. This is the only recognized form of exorcism.

Experts say that no informal exorcism should ever be attempted because demons have the ability to jump from one person or object to another or to return to the body of an individual after having left it. General demonology wisdom suggests that cases of repossession are much more difficult to resolve than original possession.

Extra-Sensory Perception - Extra sensory perception or ESP is the ability to gain insights about the motivations and actions of individuals and events in the world through senses beyond those that are considered ordinary for human abilities.

F

Fairy - A small supernatural creature with magical powers. Very small and generally female. Also known as a pixie, imp, brownie, or sprite.

Fallen Angels - The angels expelled from heaven with Satan as described in Revelation 12:7-12.

Familiar Spirit - A a familiar or a spirit of familiar is generally an animal that attends an individual for purposes of service and protection. The most common example is that of a cat serving a witch. Such a spirit can, however, assume human form as well.

Fetish - A fetish is any object to that is regarded by its holder as sacred or magical in nature.

Fortune Teller - As the name implies, and fortune teller is one who looks into the future and relates the events that are seen to inquiring individuals.

Fundamentalist - In referring to Christians, a group that holds to the literal interpretation of scripture in regard to key doctrines of their faith.

G

Ghost - The term ghost is applied generically to all types of apparitions and supernatural entities even though they may be of a different nature than the spirit of an actual deceased individual.

Gnosticism - Gnosticism was a 2nd century heretical movement in Christianity that taught a belief in the demiruge, a lesser divine being who ruled the earth, while Christ was seen as the emissary of a more remote and supreme being. In this school of thought, salvation or redemption depended on the attainment of esoteric knowledge or "gnosis."

Grimoire - A book that contains magic spells, invocations, and reference materials such as lists and descriptions of demons.

Graphology - Graphology is an attempt to analyze the character and motivations of an individual by examining samples of that person's handwriting.

Gray Magic - Grey magic is, as the name implies, a gray field in which demonic powers are appealed to for the purpose of accomplishing a goal that is not necessarily evil in intent or purpose. Clearly, this is something that should only be undertaken with extreme care.

H

Halomancy - Halomancy or "alomancy" is a type of divination in which information is sought by the use of salt.

Harry Potter - A series of seven novels in the fantasy genre written by the British author J.K. Rowling. Because the books chronicle the adventures of a young wizard at a wizarding school, they were looked at askance in some religious circles as promoting evil.

Heavenly Host - A term used in the Bible and in literature to refer to angels.

Hebrew - A member of a group of ancient people living in what is now modern-day Israel and Palestine. According to the Bible, they are descended from the patriarch Jacob, grandson of Abraham. Also a reference to the language spoken by this group.

Hebrew Bible - The term "Hebrew Bible" is a scholarly neutral term that refers to ancient Jewish writings not necessarily considered canonic for purposes of assembling the Christian or Catholic versions of the Old Testament.

Hex - Like a curse, a hex, is the use of an evil spell to bring about a desired event or to call misfortune into the life of an individual.

Holy Water - Water that has been blessed by a priest for use in religious ceremonies including the exorcism of demons.

Horoscope - A horoscope is a diagram drawn up for an individual that shows the position of the planets and stars relative to the astrological sign of the zodiac under which that person was born. It is used to give the individual insight into the direction of their lives, and is a form of divination.

I

Incubus - An incubus is a male demon that engages in sexual activity with sleeping women in order to father demonic children. The female counterpart of an incubus is a succubus.

Intelligent Haunting - An intelligent haunting is one in which the spirit present is aware of its surroundings and acts with forethought including communicating with the living to achieve specific outcomes.

L

LaVey, Anton - An American occultist and author born in Chicago in 1930 and died in San Francisco in 1997. He is the founder of the Church of Satan.

Levitation - An instance of a physical object or individual rising from a surface in defiance of the laws of gravity.

M

Magic - In terms of the supernatural, magic is the ability of a person or group to use supernatural powers activated via means of spells and incantations to exert influence over the natural forces of the world or over individuals.

Malleus Maleficarum - A treatise on the prosecution of witches by a German clergyman, Heinrich Kramer, published in 1486. The literal translation of the title is "Hammer of Witches."

Malevolent Spirit - A spirit that works with ill intent in regard to an individual, group, environment, or situation.

Materialization - The appearance, usually sudden, or a spirit, entity, or object.

Meditation - Meditation is a process by which the mind is cleared of thoughts to achieve a state of clarity either for purposes of personal benefit or to gain enlightenment from spirit guides.

Medium - A medium is an individual who acts as an intermediary between this world and the spirit world. They have the ability to communicate with spirits both benevolent and evil including demons and their voices can be used by the dead to communicate with the living in this realm.

Metaphysics - Metaphysics is the study of the world outside the perceived rules and boundaries of science. This includes the great body of esoteric thought and literature surrounding spiritual and religious questions that falls outside the realm of canonical writings, specifically those contained in the Bible.

N

Necromancy - The practice of necromancy involves conjuring the spirits of the dead for purposes of gaining information. This includes the temporary reanimation of corpses.

Nephilim - The giants who were the offspring of the "daughters of men" and the "sons of God" before the Great Flood. There are references to them in Genesis 6:4 and Numbers 13:33.

Numerology - Numerology is a branch of divination in which information is gained about an individual and their future through numerical computations based initially on the date of the persons birth.

O

Occult - The term "occult" refers to the study of and participation in a wide body of supernatural, mystical, magical, and secret powers. In popular use, especially in relation to works of fiction both written and in film, the word has come to have a negative connotation.

Omen - An omen is any phenomenon or occurrence that is believed to have significance in forecasting or portending future events.

Oneiromancy - The interpretation of dreams for purposes of insight and divination.

Ooscopy - A form of divination used wisely in Mexican esoteric practices whereby the future is foretold with eggs.

Ouija Board - A game board first introduced in the 19th century amid a wave of spiritualism following the American Civil War. At the time, grieving individuals sought desperately for a means to communicate with their dead loved ones. The board was intended to convey such messages. It has no origins in antiquity, and was never intended as it is often perceived as a means for opening the gates of hell.

P

Paranormal - Any event or phenomenon that is said to exist outside the realm of activity that can be rationally or scientifically explained.

Palmistry - A means of divination that involves examining the lines, formations, and other marks on the palms of the hands.

Phrenology - A means of divination in which the shape of the skull including the presence of any bumps or other formations is used to make judgments about character and to foretell the future.

Physiognomy - A means of character analysis based entirely upon an assessment of an individual's physical features.

Poltergeist - A poltergeist is a mischievous spirit that is said to be responsible for moving inanimate objects and causing strange noises.

Pope - The bishop of Rome and the head of the Roman Catholic Church. Also called the pontiff.

Potions - Potions are mixtures of herbs and other substances created for purposes of magic, to effect cures, to bring about desired results, or for their power to incite visions and hallucinations.

Prayer to the Archangel Michael - A specific prayer for use in an exorcism or other situations requiring protection from demons and evil spirits as formulated by Pope Leo XIII.

Precognition - Precognition is the ability to see and relate events that have not yet occurred.

Premonition - A premonition is a vision or an uneasy anticipation of an event that has not yet occurred.

Prognostication - Prognostication is the ability to foretell the future.

Prophecy - A prediction or foretelling of the future.

Protection Prayer - Any one of a number of prayers including the Prayer of Jabez and the 23rd Psalm used to protect a believer from the presence of evil.

Psychic - A psychic is a person who has a sensitivity to non-physical forces at work in the world and an ability to interpret their potential significance.

Psychic Phenomena - A psychic phenomenon is any event that cannot be explained by logical means or by specific reference to science and thus is attributed to the work of spiritual forces or agents.

Puritans - A group of English Protestants, many of whom settled in New England in the 16th and 17th century. Including, but not limited to English Calvinists.

R

Reincarnation - Reincarnation is the belief that after death the soul is reborn into a new body to live a new life. In some religions, the belief extends to the interpretation that the repeated lives exist to create a venue by which wrongdoing from previous lives or character flaws exhibited during those lives can be corrected or improved.

Residual Haunting - A residual haunting is the appearance of a spirit that is unaware of its surroundings. The haunting is akin to a recording caught in a constant loop.

Rhabdomancy - A means of divination where information is gained by use of the stick or wand.

S

Sabbat - A sabbat is a meeting of a coven of witches often to initiate new members.

Salem Witch Trials - A series of hearings of suspected witches that took place in colonial Massachusetts from February 1692 to May 1693.

Satan - Satan is chief among the angels that fell from grace during the War in Heaven. A former archangel, Satan and the angels who left the heavenly host with him seek to subvert the relationship between man and God through deception and other means of lies and trickery.

Satanism - The worship of Satan, often including a travesty of accepted Christian symbols, for instance the use of inverted crosses. Does not, however, necessarily mean the worship of the Christian devil.

Seance - A séance is a meeting of a group of people including a psychic for medium for the purpose of making contact with and communicating with spirits from the other side.

Seer - A seer is an individual who has the ability to predict future events and developments.

Seth - The brother of Osiris and Isis in Egyptian mythology. Represented all things chaotic in the world and all forces that threatened harmony.

Smudging - The burning of dried herbs, especially sage, for the purpose of distributing the smoke through an area to clean it of evil and malevolent spirits.

Soothsaying - The act of predicting future events.

Sorcerer - An alternate term for a magician, wizard or witch.

Sorcery - The act of using magical powers for the purpose of influencing or exerting individual will, altering the outcome of an event, or controlling evil spirits.

Spell - A spell is a spoken pattern of words that, if we recited correctly, is believed to have the power to create a specific outcome or to summon spirits, both benevolent and the evil.

Spiritism - Spiritualism is the belief that the souls of the dead have the ability to communicate with living individuals through the conduit of the psychic or medium.

Sprite - Another term for a fairy or elf.

St. Benedict - St. Benedict was the founder of the Benedictine order of monks. The Medals of St. Benedict are considered to be especially powerful protection against demons.

Stigmata - In the Christian tradition, marks on the body that correspond to the wounds Christ suffered during the Crucifixion.

Succubus - A succubus is a female demon that attacks men sexually in their sleep, causing their health to deteriorate to the point of death. The male counterpart is an incubus.

Supernatural - Any event or manifestation that is attributed to a force outside the realm of the laws of nature and science.

T

Tarot Cards - A deck of cards, ancient in origin, that is believed to convey the ability to foresee the future and to tell fortunes.

Telepathy - Telepathy is the ability of one mind to communicate with another outside the use of physical channels. It is, literally, thought to thought communication.

Trance - A trance is a deep meditative state often achieved by psychics, mediums, and other meditators. If sufficiently deep, a trance may be likened to a state of suspended animation. Mediums frequently enter a trance to make room for a visiting spirit to communicate through them.

W

War in Heaven - The war in heaven, as described in the Book of Revelation, was a conflict between angelic forces led by the archangel Michael and those under the command of "the dragon" of Satan. It resulted in Satan's expulsion from heaven.

Warlock - A warlock is a male witch.

White Magic - A form of magic in which powers are used only for good.

Wicca - A nature religion practiced by individuals that identify as witches and warlocks. It cannot and should not be mistaken as "devil worship" or Satanism. Wiccans revere the life force in its dual form as The Lord and The Lady.

Witch - A woman who practices magic for benevolent (White) or malevolent (Black) purposes.

Witchcraft - The practice of magic by a witch.

Wizard - An alternate term for a sorcerer or magician.

X

Xylomancy - a means of divination that seeks to predict events and foretell the future using pieces of wood.

Z

Zoroastrianism - A pre-Islamic monotheistic faith that dates to Persia in the 6th century BC.

Works Consulted

Belanger, Michelle. *The Dictionary of Demons: Names of the Damned*. Llewellyn Publications, October 2010.

Campbell, Alexander. *Demonology*. GodSpeed Publishing, 2013.

Cunningham, Scott. *Wicca: A Guide for the Solitary Practitioner*. Llewellyn Publications, October 1993.

De la Torre, Miguel. *The Quest for the Historical Satan*. Fortress Press, 2011.

Greer, John Michael. *The New Encyclopedia of the Occult*. Llewellyn Publications, October 2003.

Guiley, Rosemary Ellen and John Zaffis. *The Encyclopedia of Demons and Demonology*. Checkmark Books, August 2009.

Guiley, Rosemary. *The Encyclopedia of Angels*. Facts on File, December 2003.

Lumpkin, Joseph B. *Fallen Angels, Watchers, and the Origins of Evil*. Fifth Estate, 2007.

Mathers, Samuel Lidell MacGregor. *The Key of Solomon the King*.

Michael, Caron. *Demonology: Possession, Exorcism and the Kingdom of Darkness*.

Pagels, Elaine. *The Origin of Satan: How Christians Demonized Jews, Pagans, and Heretics.* Vintage, 2011.

Pagels, Elaine. *The Gnostic Gospels.* Random House, 2004.

Pagels, Elaine. *Revelations: Visions, Prophecy, and Politics in the Book of Revelation.* Penguin, 2012.

Partridge, Christopher H. and Eric S. Christianson. *The Lure of the Dark Side: Satan and Western Demonology in Popular Culture.* Routledge, 2014.

Peterson, Joseph H. *Grimorium Verum.* October 2007.

Schaff, Philip. *History of the Christian Church.*

Tarnas, Richard. *Passion of the Western Mind.* Ballantine Books, 2011.

Tosatti, Marco. *Memoirs of an Exorcist: My Life Fighting Satan.* Piemme, 2014.

Webster, Richard. *Encyclopedia of Angels.* Llewellyn Publications, 2009.

Young, Stephen. *Demons: True Stories of Demonic Possessions and Demonic Attacks.*

Index

Lightning Source UK Ltd.
Milton Keynes UK
UKOW06f2049240317
297487UK00005B/213/P